DATE DUE

Pebble®

Polar Animals
Caribou

by Helen Frost

Consulting Editor: Gail Saunders-Smith, PhD

Consultant: Brian M. Barnes, Director
Institute of Arctic Biology
University of Alaska, Fairbanks

Capstone
press®

Mankato, Minnesota

Pebble Books are published by Capstone Press,
151 Good Counsel Drive, P.O. Box 669, Mankato, Minnesota 56002.
www.capstonepress.com

1 2 3 4 5 6 11 10 09 08 07 06

Library of Congress Cataloging-in-Publication Data
Frost, Helen, 1949–
    Caribou / by Helen Frost.
    p. cm.—(Pebble books. Polar animals)
    Summary: "Simple text and photographs present caribou, where they live,
and what they do"—Provided by publisher.
    Includes bibliographical references and index.
    ISBN-13: 978-0-7368-4245-7 (hardcover)
    ISBN-10: 0-7368-4245-4 (hardcover)
    1. Caribou—Juvenile literature. I. Title. II. Series.
QL737.U55F76 2007
599.65'8—dc22   2004026898

Note to Parents and Teachers

The Polar Animals set supports national science standards related to
life science. This book describes and illustrates caribou. The images
support early readers in understanding the text. The repetition of
words and phrases helps early readers learn new words. This book
also introduces early readers to subject-specific vocabulary words,
which are defined in the Glossary section. Early readers may need
assistance to read some words and to use the Table of Contents,
Glossary, Read More, Internet Sites, and Index sections of the book.

Table of Contents

What Are Caribou?

Caribou are large mammals in the deer family. Caribou are sometimes called reindeer.

Caribou are
brown and white.
Thick fur keeps
them warm.

areas where caribou live

8

Where Caribou Live

Caribou herds live
in cold northern areas.
They live on the tundra
in the summer.
They live in forests
in the winter.

Body Parts

A caribou uses
its wide, flat hooves
to walk in deep snow.
Its hooves make
a clicking noise.

Caribou have
long, thin legs.
They walk far
across the tundra.

Caribou use their antlers to fight.

What Caribou Do

Caribou dig through snow to find food.
They eat leaves, berries, and grass.

Caribou herds travel
between their winter
and summer homes.
Caribou swim
across lakes and rivers
as they migrate.

Caribou herds rest together on the tundra at night.

Glossary

antler—a large, branching, bony body part on a deer's head; both male and female caribou have antlers; male caribou fight with their antlers.

deer—an animal with hooves that runs fast and eats plants

forest—a large area thickly covered with trees and plants; forests are also called woodlands.

herd—a large group of animals

hoof—the foot of a large, heavy mammal with long, thin legs, such as a horse, deer, or cow

mammal—a warm-blooded animal that has a backbone; mammals have fur or hair; female mammals feed milk to their young.

migrate—to move from one place to another when seasons change

tundra—a flat, cold area without trees; the ground stays frozen in the tundra for most of the year.

Read More

Glassman, Jackie. *Amazing Arctic Animals.* New York: Grosset & Dunlap, 2002.

Lindeen, Carol K. *Life in a Polar Region.* Pebble Plus: Living in a Biome. Mankato, Minn.: Capstone Press, 2004.

Internet Sites

FactHound offers a safe, fun way to find Internet sites related to this book. All of the sites on FactHound have been researched by our staff.

Here's how:

1. Visit *www.facthound.com*

2. Choose your grade level.

3. Type in this book ID **0736842454** for age-appropriate sites. You may also browse subjects by clicking on letters, or by clicking on pictures and words.

4. Click on the **Fetch It** button.

FactHound will fetch the best sites for you!

Index

Word Count: 120
Grade: 1
Early-Intervention Level: 15

Editorial Credits
Martha E. H. Rustad, editor; Patrick D. Dentinger, designer; Wanda Winch, photo
    researcher; Scott Thoms, photo editor

Photo Credits
Bruce Coleman Inc./Martin W. Grosnick, 14
Corbis/Galen Rowell, 20; Kennan Ward, 12; Steve Kaufman, 4
Getty Images Inc./The Image Bank/Michael Melford, 1; Stone/Daniel J. Cox, 8
Minden Pictures/John Eastcott/Yva Momatiuk, 16; Michael Mauro, cover;
    Michael Quinton, 6; Michio Hoshino, 18
Peter Arnold Inc./Steven Kazlowski, 10